IT'LL NEVER WORK

BUILDINGS, BRIDGES AND TUNNELS

JON RICHARDS

W

FRANKLIN WATTS

Franklin Watts
Published in paperback in Great Britain in 2019
by The Watts Publishing Group

Credits
Conceived, designed and edited by
Tall Tree Ltd
Editor: David John
Designer: Gary Hyde

ISBN 978 1 4451 5058 1

Printed in China

Franklin Watts
An imprint of
Hachette Children's Group
Part of The Watts Publishing Group
Carmelite House
50 Victoria Embankment
London EC4Y 0DZ

An Hachette UK Company
www.hachette.co.uk
www.franklinwatts.co.uk

Picture credits:
t-top, b-bottom, l-left, r-right,
c-centre, m-middle
All images public domain unless otherwise
indicated:
Front cover: cl Krisztian Miklosy/Dreamstime.com; c Deejpilot/
iStockphoto.com; cr Christian Bertrand/Dreamstime.com; bc
Fotokon/Dreamstime.com; br ollo/iStockphoto.com; 1c
Vitalyedush/Dreamstime.com; 2 Paul Wishart/Dreamstime.com; 3b
1971yes/Dreamstime.com; 4cr BMCL/Shutterstock.com; 4b
Ulldellebre/Dreamstime.com; 6c Vitalyedush/Dreamstime.com; 7tr
Freer Law/Dreamstime.com; 7b Tomas1111/Dreamstime.com; 8c
Stillwords/Dreamstime.com; 11c Krisztian Miklosy/Dreamstime.
com; 12c Paul Wishart/Dreamstime.com; 13t kelvinjay/iStockphoto.
com; 13b emotionart/Dreamstime.com; 14b allekk/iStockphoto.com;
15t Libux 77/Dreamstime.com; 15c Christian Bertrand/Dreamstime.
com; 15b Xin Hua/Dreamstime.com; 16br jeffplay/Dreamstime.
com; 17 cl saiko3p/Dreamstime.com; 17c Mike Clegg/Dreamstime.
com; 19bl Deejpilot/iStockphoto.com; 20c 1971yes/Dreamstime.
com; 21t stpmj; 21c Gordon Bell/Dreamstime.com; 21b AZPA; 24t
Krzysztof Przygoda/Dreamstime.com; 24c Andersastphoto/
Dreamstime.com; 26c Gettyimages; 27t Leonid Andronov/
Dreamstime.com; 28c Luca Chiartano/Dreamstime.com; 31 jeffplay/
Dreamstime.com; BACK COVER: tr 20c 1971yes/Dreamstime.com;
cr Paul Wishart/Dreamstime.com.

CONTENTS

BRICK BY BRICK

Humans have always needed shelter. When our earliest ancestors moved out of caves, they had to learn how to construct homes, using any building materials they could find or make.

TEMPORARY BUILDINGS 👉

The first shelters could be taken down and carried from place to place as people moved in search of food. The materials used were animal skins, wooden poles or even large bones. Although they allowed people to be mobile, these dwellings were often small, cold and uncomfortable.

An Aboriginal shelter, Australia

👉 BRICKS OF MUD

The first mud-brick structures were built in the Indus Valley civilisations of southern Asia from about 7000 BCE. The bricks were easy to make and offered a simple construction material in places where there was little wood to build with. They baked hard in the sun, which meant that people didn't have to collect fuel for kilns. Houses were built up to three stories high, with livestock inhabiting the ground floor.

The Great Mosque of Djenné, Mali, founded in about 1300, is the world's largest mud-brick building.

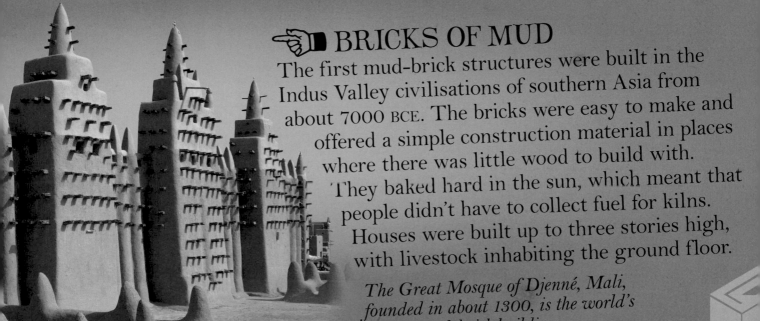

MAKING BRICKS

Mud bricks are made from a mixture of soil, mud, sand, water and something to bind the mixture together and stop it from cracking, such as straw. The materials are mixed together and then poured into a special mould. The moulds are then left out in the sun to dry and bake hard, before being knocked out and used to build a wall. For added protection, the bricks can be covered with a layer of plaster.

Mud pressed into moulds

Bricks bake in the sun

CONCRETE 👉

Concrete is a mix of cement and crushed stones called aggregate. It can be poured and moulded into shape and will dry hard to form a tough surface. Materials similar to concrete were being used in the Middle East as long ago as 6500 BCE. However, it was during the Roman Empire, from about 300 BCE to CE 476, that the use of concrete in construction was perfected. The greatest Roman concrete building is the Pantheon in Rome. The Romans found that adding horsehair made concrete less likely to crack, while mixing in animal blood stopped it crumbling in frosty weather.

The Pantheon was built in CE 126 by the emperor Hadrian. Its dome spans 43 metres, a width not exceeded until modern times.

STONE, WOOD, STEEL AND GLASS

Over time, building materials became more varied as improvements in transport allowed them to be carried from farther away. New materials led to grander designs.

👉 STONE

Building with stone can create buildings that last for thousands of years, but stone is very heavy and takes a lot of effort to transport and shape. One of the largest stone structures ever built is the Great Pyramid at Giza, Egypt. This triangle-sided building was a tomb for the pharaoh Khufu and stands 145 metres tall.

The Great Pyramid was the tallest building in the world for 3,500 years.

BUILDING THE PYRAMID

Built in about 2560 BCE, the Great Pyramid comprises 2.5 million stone blocks, each weighing about 2 tonnes. Some were transported by boat from Aswan, more than 800 km away. At the site, up to 30,000 workers dragged the stones up ramps and into place on the pyramid. The vast structure was then encased in smooth limestone.

Blocks were rolled on logs up earth ramps.

WOOD AND STRAW 👉

Until the 1700s, most homes in Europe were timber-framed. Many had roofs of straw, which was cheap and readily available. However, in tightly packed cities such as London, they could create a highly flammable environment. Disaster struck in September 1666, when fire spread through London, destroying much of the city. To prevent this happening again, laws were passed that allowed only houses of brick and stone to be built in the city.

The Great Fire destroyed whole districts of London.

This English farmhouse of the 1500s is timber-framed house with a thatched straw roof.

7

The dramatic cityscape of Shanghai, China

STEEL AND GLASS

Modern materials are lighter and stronger than traditional wood or stone. They allow engineers and architects to create amazing buildings that rise hundreds of metres into the air or form astonishing shapes. Steel, first mass-produced in the 1800s, can be used to create incredibly strong frameworks (see pages 18-19), while covering materials, such as glass, can create curves and sharp lines.

CASTLES

Early castles and forts were built from wood. They offered protection from attack, but caught fire easily. Stronger materials, such as stone, were needed, as well as clever designs that helped the inhabitants fend off an enemy.

STONE FORTRESS 👉

Krak des Chevaliers in Syria was built in the 1100s by the Knights Hospitalier, warrior monks who had conquered the region during the First Crusade in 1099. The castle was home to 2,000 knights until 1271, when it was attacked by the 10,000-strong Muslim army of Sultan Baibars. Its stone walls built in concentric rings (one ring surrounding another) allowed the knights to withstand a siege of 36 days before they surrendered.

Krak des Chevaliers stands almost intact today.

CASTLE DESIGN

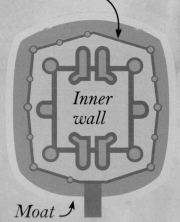

Outer wall

Inner wall

Moat ↗

Castle walls were built in concentric rings so that, if an outer ring was captured, defenders could retreat to an inner one. Inner walls were higher than outer walls, so defenders could shoot arrows down on their enemy. Battlements were crenellated (with high and low sections), so that defenders could hide and shoot.

Beaumaris Castle in Wales, built in the 1280s, has concentric rings of defensive walls and a moat.

THE COMING OF GUNPOWDER 👉

The first gunpowder weapons were made in the 1300s. They were too weak and unreliable to threaten thick castle walls. However, within 200 years, gunpowder cannons had become so powerful and accurate that castle design had to change. New features included sharply angled walls to deflect cannon balls, and thick earth banks piled up behind walls to absorb the force of an impact. Before long, however, even these innovations were not enough to withstand modern firepower, and castle-building went into decline.

An early cannon fires a shot at the castle walls during the siege of Orléans, France, in 1428.

MODERN FORTIFICATIONS

From the 1930s, fortifications were built from reinforced concrete to withstand aircraft and tank attacks. The Maginot Line and the Siegfried Line were built by France and Germany in the 1930s to defend themselves from each other. Both consisted of reinforced bunkers, tunnels and trenches. During the Second World War (1939–1945), invading German forces simply drove around the French Maginot Line. When Allied forces pushed the Germans back in 1944, the Germans found that their Siegfried Line offered little protection against the latest weapons.

Reinforced concrete defences of the Maginot Line in France.

PLACES OF WORSHIP

Every civilisation has used its most talented architects to design awe-inspiring places of worship. Some of these buildings were forgotten and neglected. Others were so ambitious they fell down or started to lean over!

GIANT STONE TEMPLES

The huge temples at Abu Simbel in Egypt were begun in 1264 BCE to celebrate the reign of Pharaoh Ramesses II. They were carved into rock and guarded by colossal statues of the pharaoh. Over the centuries, the temples were forgotten and became buried in sand. They lay hidden until 1813, when a local boy showed them to an astonished archaeologist.

The statues of Ramesses are 20 metres high.

Beauvais Cathedral in 1569 (left) and without its spire today (above).

CATHEDRAL COLLAPSE

Egypt wasn't the only place with vast temples. The Gothic churches of medieval Europe were given mighty stone spires. In 1569, a 153-metre spire made Beauvais Cathedral in France the world's tallest building. The spire was too big and too heavy. It collapsed and was not rebuilt.

FLYING BUTTRESS

Some cathedrals use an architectural feature called a flying buttress to help support the weight of their stone walls. This is a large pillar on the outside of the building with an arch at the top that joins the buttress to the building. It directs any outwards-pushing forces down into the ground.

Flying buttresses support the stone wall.

LEANING TOWERS

Sometimes, things go wrong even as a building is being constructed. Work started on the cathedral bell tower in the Italian city of Pisa in 1173. However, weak soil and poor foundations soon caused the tower to lean to one side. Work continued over the next 200 years as more floors were added, but the tower continued to lean more and more. The ground beneath it was finally made stable between 1990 and 2001. Today, the angle of lean stands at 3.99 degrees.

This church at Suurhusen in Germany was built on unstable ground. It leans at 5 degrees.

Tourists can climb the Leaning Tower of Pisa's 300 steps.

A PLACE TO LIVE

With the founding of the earliest cities about 8,000 years ago, many people settled in permanent homes. Early homes had just one room, but became more complex as building techniques and materials improved.

IRON AGE HOUSE

Early homes in northern Europe looked similar to the temporary homes of nomads. Two thousand years ago, a house had one room in which a family lived, slept and ate. The homes were round, with walls of wattle and daub (see below), and a thatched roof. There was no chimney. Smoke from a fire filtered through the thatch.

Smoke from inside helped preserve the thatch.

WATTLE AND DAUB

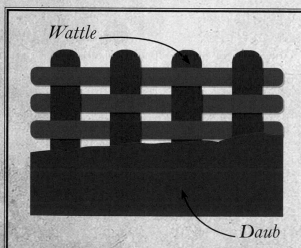

Wattle

Daub

This is a building material used to make walls. It consists of a lattice of woven wooden strips covered in a thick, sticky material, which could be a mixture of clay, soil or even dung. This dried to produce a hard exterior. Wattle and daub is still used in some buildings today.

BRICK HOUSES

In the Industrial Revolution of the 1800s, Britain saw a boom in brick-built homes to house workers near factories. Families lived in cramped spaces and vermin such as mice and bed bugs were common. An 1875 law stated that each house must have its own outside privy (toilet). Previously, slops had been thrown out with the trash.

Workers' terraced homes with outside toilets, in Cheshire, UK

HOMES IN THE SKY

After the destruction caused in Europe by the Second World War, many new homes were needed quickly and cheaply. This led to a boom in high-rise apartments. Towering apartment buildings had already been built in cities of the world where land was scarce and expensive, such as in Manhattan, New York. Today, high-rise apartment living is common. It saves space in crowded cities, and is more energy efficient than a house.

13

A modern apartment in a luxury tower block.

BUILDINGS FOR FUN

Buildings are not only places for living and working; they can be places of entertainment. These include huge sports arenas, stylish art galleries, cinemas and theatres.

THE COLOSSEUM

Built in CE 72–80, the Colosseum in Rome was a purpose-built amphitheatre that held an audience of 80,000. This oval-shaped building was built of limestone blocks held together with iron clamps rather than cement. The arena had a large wooden floor covered with sand. Beneath this were tunnels where gladiators and animals were kept during a show. The Colosseum was used to stage brutal fights. It could even be flooded to stage mock sea battles. Behind the seats were stone passages called vomitoria. These had nothing to do with vomit; they were exits through which large crowds could leave quickly.

The Colosseum's design was copied in cities all over the Roman Empire.

This replica of the Globe was built in 1997 near the original theatre's site.

THE GLOBE

Built in 1599, the Globe Theatre in London staged many of the plays of William Shakespeare. Its round shape housed an open-air stage. The audience stood to watch in front of the stage or sat in the seating that surrounded the walls. The theatre was pulled down in 1643 after religious laws banned all plays.

INSIDE-OUT BUILDING

Opened in 1971, the Centre Georges Pompidou in Paris houses a library and art gallery. It uses an innovative design to maximise the internal space – its utilities, such as pipes for power, water and heating, are all on the outside of the building, making the interior space as large as possible.

Even the escalator is on the building's exterior.

A floating football pitch extends out into the harbour.

THE FLOAT

Building space in many of today's cities is scarce. So some cities have created artificial islands for important buildings and even airports. For example, in 2007 Singapore built a stadium on its harbour, with seating for 30,000 and a platform that actually floats on the water. The arena is large enough to hold a football pitch and it can support 1,070 tonnes of weight. It is made up of smaller floating pontoons that can be rearranged for music events.

DANGER ZONES

Some areas of the world are at risk from natural disasters, such as earthquakes, volcanic eruptions and floods. Architects have found ways of creating buildings that can survive these events.

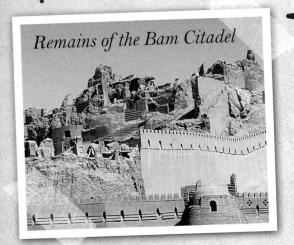

Remains of the Bam Citadel

SHAKY GROUND

Earthquakes can shake a building apart in seconds. In 2003, a violent quake in Iraq caused the collapse of the ancient Bam Citadel, which was made from a fragile material called adobe (compacted earth and straw). To protect adobe buildings, a special plastic mesh can be fitted to the building to stop the walls from cracking.

SKYSCRAPER PROTECTION

Earthquake damage is reduced if a tall building doesn't sway too much during a tremor. Engineers discovered that suspending a huge weight inside a building reduces its sway. As the building swings one way during a quake, the weight swings the other way to reduce the wobbling. Taipei 101 in Taiwan is in a quake-prone area. It is fitted with a massive 660-tonne steel-ball pendulum.

Suspended pendulum weight inside Taipei 101

BASE ISOLATORS

One of the most common ways to protect a building during an earthquake is to use base isolators. These bearings or pads separate the building from the ground, allowing the ground to move while the building stays still or moves only a little.

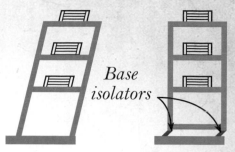

Base isolators

Building without isolators

Building with isolators

FLOODING

More than 40 per cent of people in the world live on coasts. Many of these places as well as places near rivers are prone to flooding, either during storms or rainy seasons. Architects have developed ways of taking houses out of water's way, such as raising them on stilts, or stopping floodwaters reaching areas.

Stilt houses on Vietnam's Mekong River

The Thames Barrier in London is a huge gate that closes in the event of a flood.

LIVING WITH LAVA

For thousands of years, people have chosen to live near the slopes of volcanoes because the ashy soil is very fertile for growing crops. However, these can be dangerous places to live. Little can be done to protect a house from an advancing lava flow, but there are ways of minimising other damage. For example, houses' roofs can be reinforced against the huge volumes of ash and rock that can fall during an eruption.

A house heaped with volcanic ash from Mount Pinatubo, in the Philippines, 1991

TOWERING GIANTS

When space is hard to come by, one solution is to build up into the air, creating towering skyscrapers, the tallest of which can be more than 800 metres high.

A medieval painting imagines the Tower of Babel, which rose so high it touched heaven.

👉 TOWER OF BABEL

The Bible tells of a vast tower built by the peoples of the world as a symbol of their power. Scholars believe the tower may have been the Great Ziggurat built in Babylon (in present-day Iraq) in about 2000 BCE. The Ziggurat, a stepped structure, was 90 metres tall.

GOING UP ...

Elisha Otis

Very tall buildings were not practical without safe lifts (elevators). Before Elisha Otis demonstrated his 'safety elevator' in New York in 1854, a lift could plunge to the ground if its cables snapped. Otis's lift had a brake to stop it falling. The audience at his demonstration gasped as the cable was cut, but the lift did not fall.

Otis's successful demonstration

STEEL FRAMES

Another of the key steps in skyscraper engineering was the development of an interior steel frame. A steel frame is light and strong and can support the weight of a great many floors. They are also quick to put up. In the early 1900s, skyscrapers appeared at an astonishing rate, especially in New York City.

A riveter works on the steel frame for the Empire State Building high above New York City in 1931.

PROBLEMS 👉

While skyscrapers provide planners with more floor space in a cramped city, they also present their own problems. On 15 November 2010, a fire in a tower block in Shanghai, China, spread quickly through the building after welding sparks set fire to scaffolding. It took 80 fire engines to put out the blaze, but 53 people died. After that, the city cracked down on careless building work.

The fire was put out after firemen set up water hoses atop nearby towers.

THE TALLEST OF THEM ALL 👉

In 2009, the Burj Khalifa tower in Dubai became the world's tallest building, with 154 usable floors. However, this giant of the building world will be dwarfed by the Jeddah Tower in Saudi Arabia. When it is completed in 2020, it will rise to a record-breaking 1,008 metres – more than a kilometre high!

Burj Khalifa (830 m)

Jeddah Tower (1,008 m)

FUTURE BUILDINGS

Architects dream of the next generation of buildings. These may be fantastical futuristic towers, regenerated old buildings or buildings hidden so that they don't spoil a beautiful view.

CITIES IN THE SKY 👉

Future building materials may include self-healing concrete that can repair cracks, composite materials using microscopic fibres that create super-strong structures, and shapes created using 3-D printing technology. These will allow architects to create buildings with amazing and unusual designs.

An imagined future tower

Rotating floors create dynamic shapes.

ROTATING TOWER

The Dynamic Tower will be completed in 2020 in Dubai. The floors rotate independently, completing a full rotation in 90 minutes and giving every apartment a view of the surroundings. Each floor is being built in modules and then assembled on-site, making construction of the tower faster and easier.

NOW YOU SEE IT ... 👉

No one wants to spoil an area of natural beauty, such as a national park, but what if you have to put a building there? One solution is to cover a building in mirrors. This is cheaply done as the mirrors can be fitted to existing buildings, allowing them to disappear by reflecting their surroundings.

Can you see this barn hidden by mirrors in a park?

AS GOOD AS NEW 👉

How can old buildings be given a new lease of life? One idea for this concrete power plant (below) in Germany is to cover its outside with a new covering of plants. This has the advantage of making an ugly building beautiful as well as absorbing emissions from the power plant. Other plans have seen former factories and warehouses transformed into apartments, shops and even art galleries.

The Tate Modern gallery in London is housed in an old power station.

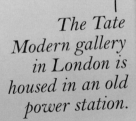

BRIDGING THE GAP

Bridges are designed to cross obstacles, such as a river or a gaping gorge. Over the years, many different designs have evolved to work with the location, the materials to hand and the technology available.

Roman troops crossing a bridge made of boats.

FLOATING BRIDGES

Pontoon bridges use boats to support a temporary deck across a river. They are often used in wartime because they are quick to build and can support heavy loads and even tanks. Pontoon bridges were regularly used in the Roman Empire. In CE 37, the mad emperor Caligula wasted a fortune to build a 5-kilometre-long pontoon bridge over the Bay of Baiae, Italy. He wanted to ride his horse on the water!

Modern replica of an Inca rope bridge.

ROPE BRIDGES

In the 1400s, the Inca Empire was spread across the Andes Mountains of South America. Bridges of woven rope and wooden slats were built to cross chasms on foot. To keep the bridges usable, local villagers had to repair them annually.

ARCHES

The Romans were some of the first people to use arches in bridges. True arches direct the weight and pressure down the sides of the arch and into the bridge's supports, or abutments. At the top of the arch is the keystone. This is the last piece of the arch put into place and it locks the other stones together.

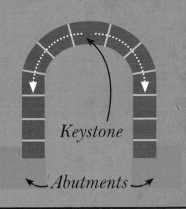

Keystone

Abutments

USING STONE

Stone provides a strong material to create long-lasting bridges. Stone bridges have been built for thousands of years, but the first true masters of bridge-building were the Romans. More than 900 Roman stone bridges still stand today. The Alcántara Bridge in Spain, for example, was completed in CE 106 and is made up of six arches stretching for more than 180 metres.

The Alcántara Bridge was so well built it is still in use after 2,000 years.

LONDON BRIDGE

In the 1100s, London Bridge was 270 metres long and formed of 19 stone arches. It was also covered in buildings — 130 shops, as well as toilets that emptied into the river. The buildings crowded the bridge, making it hard to cross. The number of supports also trapped debris in the river. The bridge stood for 600 years before being replaced by a bridge with just five arches in 1824.

Old London Bridge

AMAZING BRIDGES

Modern bridges use the latest materials, such as steel and reinforced concrete, as well as cutting-edge designs, to span ever bigger gaps in new and inventive ways.

GALLOPING GERTIE

Opened in July 1940, a new suspension bridge (see below) that crossed the Tacoma Narrows in Washington State, USA, earned the name 'Galloping Gertie' after it started twisting violently in high winds. Four months later, the bridge shook itself apart. The new bridges have struts to reduce vibrations and gaps in the road to let wind through.

Two new bridges now span the Tacoma Narrows.

SUSPENSION BRIDGES

Suspension bridges support a deck using cables attached to tall towers. The deck's weight pulls down on the cables. This force is directed to the towers and then down into the ground where the towers are anchored.

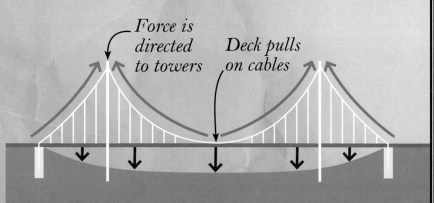

Force is directed to towers

Deck pulls on cables

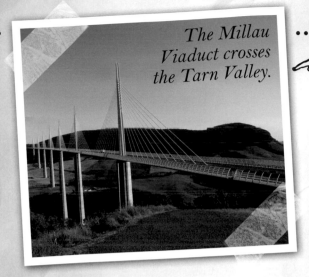

The Millau Viaduct crosses the Tarn Valley.

TOWERING BRIDGE

Located in southwest France, the Millau Viaduct opened in 2004 and is the world's tallest bridge. Its towers are 343 metres tall – taller than the Eiffel Tower. The road deck is shaped like an upside-down wing to create downforce, similar to the wing of a racing car. In strong winds, the road deck is pushed down, keeping it stable.

WOBBLY BRIDGE

The Millennium Bridge in London closed on the day it opened in June 2000, after it started wobbling. The bridge was built using cables that ran along the sides to avoid blocking the views. However, footsteps started small wobbles, which caused people to fall into step with each other and this made the wobbling worse. The solution was to add shock-absorbers.

The wobbling bridge closed for two years while modifications were made.

This artificial island is an entrance to one of the crossing's tunnels.

SPANNING THE PEARL

The Chinese cities of Hong Kong, Macau and Zhuhai sit on the Pearl River Delta. In 2009, construction began on an enormous 50-kilometre-long bridge designed to link these three cities. The crossing itself is actually made up of a series of bridges and tunnels, as well as artificial islands.

TUNNELS IN CITIES

We dig tunnels to carry objects and utilities through obstacles. Tunnels beneath city streets allow trains, gas, electricity and sewage to move quickly and conveniently.

THE BIG STINK 👉

Before the invention of proper waste systems, raw sewage was dumped directly into rivers or the sea. In London in the 1800s, the amount of sewage emptied into the River Thames became so great that it caused outbreaks of deadly cholera, and created such a bad smell that people referred to the hot summer of 1858 as 'The Big Stink'. To solve this problem, British engineer Joseph Bazalgette was commissioned in the 1860s to build a network of sewage pipes and tunnels that pumped the sewage far downriver and away from the city centre. His pipes and tunnels are still in use today.

Engineers inspect a junction in the London sewer system, built in the 1860s.

Cholera (shown as Death) rowing on the Thames.

METRO SYSTEMS 👉

As cities have expanded, so too has the traffic on their streets. One way to ease city congestion was to build underground metro systems, using trains to shuttle people around. The earliest appeared in London in the 1860s, but building them was a messy and disruptive business. Early metro tunnels in London and Paris were built using a cut-and-cover technique. A huge trench was dug, the tunnels were set in place and then the whole thing was covered over again. The first London underground train carriages had gas lighting and no windows, so a boy at each station would call out the stop. Until electric trains replaced steam trains in the 1890s, tunnels would fill with smoke.

A passenger walkway tunnelled in rock in the Stockholm Metro.

Workers building the Paris metro in the 1860s.

CROSSING A CITY

The Crossrail project is the construction of a vast network of tunnels running right across London from east to west. It is scheduled to open in 2018. Giant tunnel boring machines (TBMs) are being used to dig the tunnels. They weave their way around existing tunnels and obstacles with pinpoint accuracy. At one point, a tunnel had to go over an underground railway tunnel and under an escalator tunnel with just 1 metre to spare – a move that engineers described as going 'through the needle'.

The front of a Crossrail tunnel boring machine

GOING UNDERGROUND

As well as carrying transport and utilities under cities, tunnels are used to go under stretches of water that are too wide for bridges, to pass through mountains or to protect people and objects from attack.

Entry to the tunnel at Folkestone, England

👉 CHANNEL TUNNEL

Opened in 1994, the Channel Tunnel is a rail link connecting the UK and France. It is one of the longest undersea tunnels in the world and huge TBMs took six years to dig the 50.5-kilometre-long tunnels. A design for a tunnel was first made in the 1800s, but only with modern TBMs was the project feasible.

DIGGING THE CHANNEL TUNNEL

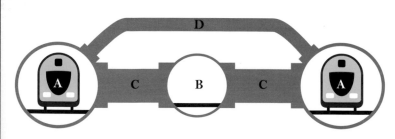

A: train tunnels; B: emergency escape tunnel;
C: escape corridor; D: service duct

During construction, 11 TBMs were used, digging tunnels from both the French and UK sides. Together, these machines weighed 12,000 tonnes. One remains buried beneath the Channel, as it was too hard to retrieve.

TUNNEL THROUGH THE ALPS

The Mont Blanc Tunnel is a 12-km road tunnel. It runs through one of the tallest mountains in Europe, linking France and Italy. In 1999, a truck in the tunnel caught fire. The fire spread and killed 38 people who were trapped by the flames and smoke. The disaster led to major changes to the tunnel, including extra security bays where trapped people can take refuge, a fire station in the middle of the tunnel and computerised fire detection equipment.

Entrance to the Mont Blanc Tunnel

NUCLEAR BUNKER

The control centre of the Cheyenne Mountain bunker system

Beneath the towering peak of Cheyenne Mountain in Colorado, USA, an enormous military command base has been tunnelled. Buried beneath more than 600 metres of granite rock, this underground facility is protected from nuclear attack and is even built on 1,000 massive springs to reduce the impact of any tremors during an earthquake. The base contains sleeping areas and suites, a medical facility, a shop, a cafeteria and fitness centres, as well as huge 25-tonne doors that are designed to survive a nuclear blast.

GLOSSARY

ABUTMENT
A structure built to support the pressure and weight of an arch or span, for example at either end of a bridge.

AMPHITHEATRE
An oval or circular building with seating surrounding a central area where events – such as gladiatorial contests – are staged. Amphitheatres were common throughout the Roman Empire.

ARCHITECT
Someone who designs buildings.

BATTLEMENTS
The walls around the top of a castle.

BUTTRESS
A structure used to reinforce another, usually larger, structure.

CIVILISATION
An advanced human society.

CONCENTRIC
Fitting completely inside something of the same shape.

CONCRETE
A building material made from a moist mixture of sand, gravel, water and cement that dries to become rock hard.

FLAMMABLE
Can easily catch fire.

FORTIFICATIONS
Structures, such as a wall, ditch or moat, added to improve a building's defences, such as those of a castle.

FOUNDATIONS
The parts of a building that bear most of the weight. They are usually located below the ground.

GLADIATOR
A person who took part in public battles against other people (or animals) during entertainments in ancient Rome.

GUNPOWDER
An explosive powder made from a mix of saltpetre, sulphur and charcoal. Gunpowder was invented in China about 1,000 years ago.

INDUSTRIAL REVOLUTION

The transformation from an agricultural economy to a mechanised, manufacturing economy that began in the UK in about 1750.

KILN

An oven for drying and hardening clay or mud.

MEDIEVAL

Relating the Middle Ages, the period of European history that lasted from roughly CE 600 to 1500.

PYRAMID

A large stone structure with a square base and triangular sides used as a tomb for kings in ancient Egypt.

SIEGE

A military campaign in which an army surrounds a city or town and cuts off its supplies in order to try and get it to surrender.

SKYSCRAPER

A very tall building that has many floors.

SPIRE

A pointed, conical structure on top of a building, such as a church or tower.

INDEX